LUCKY
EVERY DAY

LUCKY EVERY DAY

THE WISDOM OF DIANE GEPPI-AIKENS

❖

20 UNFORGETTABLE LESSONS FROM A COACH WHO MADE A DIFFERENCE

❖

CHIP SILVERMAN

WARNER BOOKS

NEW YORK   BOSTON

Warner Books

Time Warner Book Group
1271 Avenue of the Americas, New York, NY 10020
Visit our Web site at www.twbookmark.com.

Printed in the United States of America

First Printing: April 2004

10 9 8 7 6 5 4 3 2 1

Library of Congress Cataloging-in-Publication Data

Silverman, Chip.
    Lucky every day : 20 unforgettable lessons from a coach who made a difference /
Chip Silverman.
        p. cm.
        ISBN 0-446-50013-5
    1. Lacrosse for women—Coaching—United States—Anecdotes. 2. Geppi-Aikens,
Diane, 1962–2003. 3. Women coaches (Athletics)—United States—Conduct of life.
I. Title.
    GV989.15.S55 2004
    796.34'7'082—dc22

                                                          2003025805

Book design and text composition by L&G McRee

To the memory of Diane Geppi-Aikens,
an inspiration to us all

ACKNOWLEDGMENTS

First, special thanks to Warner Books for their generous contribution to Diane's children's trust.

More thanks to Caryn Karmatz Rudy, Senior Editor at Warner Books, for developing and spearheading the idea for an inspirational book about Diane Geppi-Aikens; and to my agent, Ira Rainess, for representing the Geppi-Aikens family pro bono, and for bringing me into this project.

Also, my gratitude to Renée Silverman for her excellent editing and insight on this book, under a very tight deadline; and to Eileen Lesser, Delene Carlee, Patti Gorsuch, and Susan Flaherty for their much needed assistance.

I can't thank the Loyola College women's lacrosse coaching staff of Keri Johnson, Krystin Porcella, and Stacey Morlang enough for their tireless guidance and enlightening stories; or Janine Tucker and Sara Day for their invaluable background and research input.

Finally, heartfelt thanks to the following individuals whose reflections and anecdotes contributed to the fabric of

Lucky Every Day: Natalie Sherman, John and Katherine Geppi, Terri Price, Kate Plantholt, Krissy Warnock, Kristi Korrow, Caroline Cooper, Sara Shoaf, Sarah Hannan, Michelle Batza-Railey, Mary Hart-Gagnon, Katie Hart-Mangione, Maureen A. "Mo" Duffy, Andrea Borowski, Robyn Kirby, Jenifer Albright, Patricia Grant, Carmen Pineyro, Patti Geppi-Gorsuch, Joanina Krosnowski. Trish Dabrowski, and Kory Miller.

CONTENTS

INTRODUCTION

···❖···

Diane Geppi-Aikens had three wishes in December 2002: to see her son, Michael, graduate from high school in June 2003; to see and coach the Loyola College women's lacrosse team to the Final Four lacrosse championships; and to finally see her team on national television. These may sound like accomplishments well within the grasp of a woman whose son was a high school senior in good standing, and whose team had spent most of the season ranked number one in the country. But this was no ordinary woman: In December 2002, her doctors informed Diane Geppi-Aikens that the brain tumors she had been fighting valiantly for the past seven and a half years were no longer treatable. She had terminal brain cancer, and could hope to live only a few more weeks.

Her doctors should have known better. Diane Geppi-Aikens's determination, intensity, sheer grit, and pure and unadulterated love for life were incomparable, and these attributes, coupled with the fierce love and loyalty of family, friends, and a team that knew this season would be their coach's last, were forces to be reckoned with. Diane dug in, as she had throughout her short but legendary career, and lived to see all three of her wishes come true. It was a miraculous year, and although she came short of winning the national championship outright, she won so much more: the adoration and adulation of not only sports fans and lacrosse fans nationwide, but also the general public through heartbreaking coverage in national publications such as *Sports Illustrated, USA Today,* and the *Washington Post,* and on shows like the *Today* show, *CBS Evening News with Dan Rather, NBC Nightly News with Tom Brokaw,* ESPN's *SportsCenter,* College Sports TV, *Good Morning America,* and many others where she and her players brought tears to the eyes of even the most hard-hearted viewers.

So who was this remarkable woman, arguably the best lacrosse coach in the history of the game, who inspired and led so many? Diane Marie Geppi-Aikens was born on October 4, 1962, to John and Katherine Geppi. One of three children, Diane became interested in sports when she was very young. She loved to compete and could frequently be found throwing and catching balls. From the time she was seven years old, she played ball in the alleys or at the park with her friends. She joined the Baltimore County Bureau of Recreation teams when she was in elementary school.

"When the weather was bad," Katherine Geppi remembers, "she would run up and down the stairs inside the house until we thought she would wear them out."

Although Diane played just about every sport, her favorite—and the one at which she excelled—was basketball. Interestingly, at that time, Diane was the only girl on the boys' football and baseball teams. "We always encouraged her to do whatever she wanted to do, never realizing how it would escalate," John Geppi explains.

Diane was rather small, which earned her the nickname "Shorty," but she was cat-quick and very skilled at basketball. At the time, her next-door neighbor was a baseball agent who represented several Baltimore Orioles pitchers, including Tim Stoddard, a former basketball great at North Carolina State University. One afternoon, Stoddard was outside shooting baskets on the agent's court. Some of the neighborhood kids were boasting to Stoddard that their friend Shorty could probably outshoot him. Stoddard ordered the kids to find her and bring her to the court. Diane arrived, and she and Stoddard began a foul-shooting competition. Stoddard shot first, making twenty-four of his twenty-five foul shots. Then Diane shot twenty-five out of twenty-five. Stoddard walked off the court in a huff. He couldn't believe a little twelve-year-old girl had beaten him.

At Parkville Senior High School in Baltimore County, Diane excelled in volleyball, basketball, and lacrosse. She was such an outstanding player that she made the All-Metro

Team in every one of those sports. Yet as talented as she was, she was equally unselfish. She would steal the ball, wait for her teammates to come down the court, and then hand them the ball so they could make a basket.

By her senior year, Diane had been offered more than eight scholarships, mainly for basketball, from colleges around the country. She decided to attend Loyola because she wanted to stay close to home and be with her family. Loyola wanted Diane for every sport that she played: basketball, lacrosse, and volleyball. Her parents convinced her, however, that she might have trouble maintaining her grades if she were to compete in all three sports. So Diane decided to participate just in volleyball and lacrosse, since she would have a break in the winter to catch up on her studies.

Diane started all four years of college in volleyball and lacrosse and was a two-time captain in both sports at Loyola. After her sophomore year, she suffered a nerve injury in her back that prevented her from retaining her high-scoring offensive efficiency. She refused to stop playing and switched to the position of goalkeeper, which required hardly any running. For the next two years, she won All-American honors. She still holds the record for the highest percentage of saves by a goalie at Loyola. Later, she became a two-time member of the gold-medal–winning U.S. lacrosse team. Two years after she graduated in 1984, Diane became the youngest person ever inducted into the Loyola College Athletic Hall of Fame.

In June 1984, Diane married Bob Aikens. Father Joseph Sellinger, then president of Loyola College, gave Bob some advice at the wedding: "You let Diane [whom he referred to as his "little Olympian"] continue in sports."

Right after graduation, Diane was named head volleyball coach, becoming the youngest National Collegiate Athletic Association (NCAA) Division I coach in the country at that time. She was also named assistant lacrosse coach and served in that capacity for five years until being named head lacrosse coach in 1989.

She was adored by her players, and took the school to two NCAA Final Four tournaments in her first six years of coaching. Then out of the blue came unexplained seizures. Diane, never one to worry, ignored them for months. After a particularly frightening episode on the field, however, in which Diane fell and almost broke her collarbone, Loyola's head trainer insisted that she see a doctor. Tests revealed a tumor that had been growing quietly on her brain.

After her first surgery (she would go on to have three), Diane guided tiny Loyola College to eight straight NCAA tournament berths, five Final Fours, and one NCAA final; was a three-time Intercollegiate Women's Lacrosse Coaches Association (IWLCA) National Coach of the Year; was a three-time Colonial Athletic Association Coach of the Year; was a two-time South Regional Coach of the Year; was inducted into the U.S. Lacrosse Greater Baltimore Hall of Fame; was presented the NCAA Inspiration Award; and missed only one game during that entire period of time, despite the surgeries, treatments, medication side effects, and physical handicaps.

Despite Diane's numerous sports accomplishments, she did not display an award, plaque, or trophy anywhere in her home. To learn anything about Diane's successes, you had to ask her mom and dad. The same held true for Diane's brain tumor and battle with cancer. Conversing with her on the phone or in person, it was impossible to detect that she was in the final stages of terminal cancer or even sick.

But Diane was getting sicker. Yet despite suffering many bad days from an illness that was rapidly draining her, and steroid medication that dramatically bloated her normally petite frame; despite declining from walking normally, to using a cane and then a walker, to propelling herself in a wheelchair, she missed only one game in her final season.

As her condition deteriorated, the wheelchair-bound coach was constantly questioned as to whether she could guide the team. Diane quickly and loudly responded, "I have one good leg and arm, but most importantly, my mouth still works!" She saw no point in dwelling on the bad when there was so much she still had going for her.

"Diane couldn't understand why she was selected to receive the NCAA Inspiration Award," says John. "She said to me, 'Dad, I didn't do anything yesterday differently than I did today, and I won't do anything differently tomorrow than I'm doing today.'"

What was it that was so different about Diane Geppi-Aikens that spurred her teams to such success and made such a lasting impact on all who came in contact with her? How did she deal so effectively with thirty-five young adults between eighteen and twenty-two years of age while single-handedly raising Michael, Jessica, Melissa, and Shannon, her four school-age children? How did she inspire, develop, guide, and motivate so many different personalities? And how did she do this given the many obstacles she faced?

Anyone who's played a sport can coach a team once the players hit the field. Was Diane a Vince Lombardi/Bobby Knight/Phil Jackson/Eddie Robinson type of coach? No, she was unique. She was Diane. She was inspirational, demanding (of herself and her players), focused, under-standing, and self-sacrificing. She was also a practical joke-ster, a storyteller, and a substitute mom. And she managed all of this with a calm intensity. What separates the great coaches from the average ones are the skills and qualities that get players *to* the field, keep them there, and carry over after the last game has been played. These skills and quali-ties are motivation, innovation, communication, charisma, tenacity, inspiration, a sense of humor, honesty, trust, loyalty, and the ability to serve as mentor and psychologist.

Her players flocked to her, doing all they could to make her final season one worth living by playing their hardest on the field as well as caring for her during their off-time. They thought nothing of devoting all their free time to the woman who had given so much to them over the years.

A parent of one of Diane's players stopped John Geppi in the Loyola parking lot after a game one day. "I only have one daughter, John," he said, "and your daughter has taught her more about life than she will ever learn in this college or anywhere else she goes."

This grateful parent was just one of the many I heard about who treasured the bits of wisdom and strength Diane passed on. So many players and family and friends felt touched by this incredible woman that it seemed vital to share her teachings with the world beyond Loyola's little campus. For Diane's lessons extend far beyond the lacrosse field—her teachings offer perspectives on family, friends, jobs . . . in short, how to live life right, how to live as if each day is your last, and to feel lucky every day you are on this earth. In these pages, you will be inspired by her advice on perseverance, passion, and much, much more. Please let her unique wisdom work its magic on you, for through this book, and through the many lives she has touched, Diane Geppi-Aikens's legacy will live on forever.

LUCKY
EVERY DAY

IT'S NOT THE WORDS AND MUSIC, IT'S THE PASSION

KRISTIN'S STORY

Coach Diane came out to practice one afternoon and stood watching us. We continued our drills, waiting for her next directive, until one by one we noticed that she was just staring at us with a quizzical look on her face.

We had completed three grueling days of lifting, conditioning, and practice, and now we were simply going through the motions—with no fire to play or desire to compete hard against each other.

"Get over here!" she commanded, and we ran toward her, waiting for a critique of the last passing pattern. But instead she looked around the circle of faces and quietly demanded, "What are you passionate about?"

We squirmed a bit, until it became apparent that she really wanted serious answers. As we started around the circle, many of my teammates offered words like *pets,*

KRISTIN "HAGS" HAGERT *was a starting defender at Loyola College from 1997 to 2001. She graduated as a first-team All-CAA Conference and summa cum laude (English/journalism major) in 2001. Hags went abroad for one year to coach lacrosse and teach in England. She is now the first assistant lacrosse coach at the College of William & Mary in Williamsburg, Virginia, taking graduate courses in higher education.*

friends, or *lovers;* a few said nothing. After thinking a bit, I said, "Family." Another player blurted out, "I'm passionate about being a part of a winning team!" Only three players said they were passionate about lacrosse. Diane shook her head sadly, and sent us packing for the day.

The next afternoon, we were summoned to the locker room before practice, where Diane stood next to the stereo system. We sat quietly as she began preaching: "You need to have passion in your life in order to enjoy yourself, reach your dreams, and accomplish the things you are aiming for. I'm passionate about holding a newborn baby, coaching lacrosse, and spending time with my family."

Diane insisted we understand her passions—not just her family, kids, and the game of lacrosse, but music and nature, too. She made us close our eyes and hear the singers she was passionate about: Roberta Flack and Aretha Franklin.

"Listen to the joy in their voices and hear how they sound," urged Diane. "It's not the words or the music. They sing with such great passion; such heart and soul. You can feel how the singers love what they are doing. It's not just a job to them. They're certainly not just going through the motions. If you want to excel, you need to be passionate! Otherwise, why waste your time?"

Because we were already so aware of her passion for lacrosse, Coach shared her passion for music. And somehow this exercise brought it home to us: If we wanted to excel, we had to be passionate about what we did. Diane pounded this lesson home throughout the next several weeks, focusing now on the natural beauty around us.

"Look at that sunset!" Diane would exclaim; or "What a beautiful sunrise!" (during 6 AM conditioning drills); or "See how the leaves have changed color?" She did not want us to take anything for granted. "Don't miss the little things— cherish them," she pleaded.

"Why do you give me sixteen hours a week if you're not passionate about this sport and this program?" she often asked. It made us truly evaluate our passions in life and our love for the game.

That night, many of us, including me, called our families to tell them we loved them. I was passionate about my family, and felt I needed to tell them right away. And I was passionate about lacrosse, so I was going to put forth my best effort from now on.

We played with passion for the rest of the season. It became a seasonal theme and another one of Diane's life lessons: "You must feel passion for what you do every day in order to feel success in your accomplishments and happiness in life."

I learned from Diane that a life without passion simply isn't worth the time or energy, so I've come to isolate the things that are important to me, and pursue them with vigor and passion. I've lived more happily—and more fully—ever since.

ALWAYS MAKE THE TIME

MEGAN'S STORY

The job of a head coach, no matter what sport, is more than full time. Sure, there's the regular coaching duties: running practices, coming up with strategy for games, overseeing a full staff and a full team of rambunctious college students, appearing at school fund-raising functions . . . more tasks than there are hours in the day. Despite the constant demands of her schedule, however—not to mention the responsibilities of being a single parent to four kids— Diane always managed to free her schedule, to do the things that made a difference to those around her. Rather than being a "business-as-usual" type of coach, she found the time to learn about our individual feelings and fears.

When I was much younger, my father had passed away in a plane crash. It was a very painful memory that always surfaced before I boarded a plane. Since being a varsity athlete meant lots of travel, I had to deal with these feelings a lot.

MEGAN SANTACROCE, *who played lacrosse at Loyola College from 1997 to 2001, lives in Annapolis, Maryland. An outstanding, high-scoring attacking midfielder, she was CAA Rookie of the Year, All-CAA Conference, and an All-American. Ms. Santacroce is in her second year of graduate school at Loyola, where she studies speech pathology.*

I never told Diane about this, but because she made it her business to know every significant detail in her players' lives, she found out. On one of my first team trips, we were preparing to fly to an annual lacrosse tournament, and Diane was busily trying to keep the team together and talk to airline personnel at the same time. In the midst of it all, Diane approached me and asked, concerned, "Are you okay to fly today? Do you want to sit with me?" It might have seemed a small kindness to someone like Diane, who was caring for so many people, but it meant so much to me that she took the time to look after me personally. And it made my trip—and the weekend that followed—much easier for me.

Diane's caring ways extended into my very difficult sophomore year. When I barged into her office crying one day, she dropped everything to listen and try to help me. Even when she was on the phone recruiting a player, she would stop and put my feelings and fears ahead of her many other obligations.

During the last semester of my sophomore year, I ended up needing an emergency appendectomy. While I was in the hospital in Annapolis, worrying about missing all my exams and preseason games, Diane showed up to visit. She sat with me and held my hand as I told her how painful it was for me to talk and breathe after the surgery.

"I'm going to make you laugh even if it hurts," she threatened, "because you need to laugh. Everything will be just fine. You'll see." As she spoke, a calmness came over me. I trusted her, and as usual, she was there when I needed her. She spent her precious free time with me in the hospital, when she could have been elsewhere.

But Diane was best at making time for fun. The night before playing in the title game at the 2001 Colonial Athletic Association Conference Championship in Richmond, Virginia, we all went out to dinner. The restaurant had an exciting sports bar with a band and karaoke machine. Because Diane knew that college students loved social gatherings, loud music, and dancing, she saw the opportunity to relieve some of the pressure we were feeling over the impending game. After we finished eating, Diane led us to the band and quickly climbed up onto the stage.

Instead of announcing in her solemn voice, *Girls, it's time to go now; we've got to rest up for the big game,* she grabbed the microphone and started singing the words to "It's Raining Men." Then she pulled one of the players' fathers up on stage to dance with her. We thought it was such a cool thing that our head coach would allow us to let loose. She became one of us in an instant, and it made us want to play and try even harder for her.

The hours flew by as we watched our head coach singing her heart out. Our team closed the place that night, and interestingly enough, we won the game the next morning. Diane knew that before pushing her players to the limit in a big game, it was valuable to let them blow off steam. She was well aware that the high from having fun could outweigh the benefits of a good night's sleep every once in a while.

After I graduated from college, Diane still sacrificed her time for me as she encouraged me to pursue my career goals. I was uncertain and nervous about being admitted to graduate school and pursuing a career as a speech pathologist. I didn't know which school would be the best for me, and I was reluctant to ask my former professors to write so many recommendations. When I expressed my doubts to Diane, she brushed them aside. "Go for it!" she insisted. "I'll write you all the recommendations you need." I went for it, and was accepted to six different graduate schools.

Although Diane fought some very tough battles in life, and had so much physical and mental suffering, she made time for others to the very end. Four days before she died, it was my privilege and turn to sit by her bedside and feed her ice cream. Instead of worrying and crying, or at the very least conserving her energy, she was smiling and asking me questions about my family. I had thought I was making time to be with her when it counted, but there she was, making time for me, and all her other players, family, and friends, just like she always did.

I often remember Diane's gift of making time when I find myself asked to do the same for friends, family, and other students who are struggling with obstacles in their lives. What I learned from Diane is that taking the time to make others feel good about themselves and enjoy themselves enriches both their lives and your own. Making time was Diane's greatest gift, and I hope to carry on this tradition my whole life, too.

MAKE LIFE A CHALLENGE, AND MAKE IT FUN!

LIZ'S STORY

Every lacrosse coach—and, I'm sure, every coach—on the planet wants the members of her team to push themselves to the limit, to run faster, score more goals, make more accurate passes. For Diane, though, challenging yourself wasn't only a matter of trying to improve your athletic ability. She wanted us to push ourselves to improve our lives, not just our games. She believed that the bigger the challenge before you, the more likely you would rise to meet it, and even beat it.

One challenge that Diane set up for us was the dreaded 6 AM practice. These horrifyingly early practices and runs around the dark, cool campus rose garden were a major shock to my system as a freshman at Loyola. To most of us, it was unnatural and inhumane to wake up so soon after going to sleep. Surely, coaches must have known that college students seldom slept! There were parties to attend, and

---

ELIZABETH "LIZ" SCHAFFNER *is in her sixth year as assistant coach at George Mason University in Fairfax, Virginia. Liz played for Loyola from 1994 to 1998, and was a member of the Loyola team that finished as runner-up for the national championship in 1997. She is also attending graduate school in counseling and development.*

even when there weren't, there was always someone in the dorm doing things to prevent us from getting a decent night's rest.

And our fearless leader, the woman who set the practice time, would be there right alongside us. I used to hope that the coach would not be there, and practice would be canceled. The upperclassmen informed me, however, that nothing stopped Diane from showing up. In fact, they told me that the year before, while they were complaining about running around as the sun came up, a very pregnant Diane, suffering from morning sickness, would be throwing up in the trash cans she'd placed around the field while urging them to run more and more wind sprints. They were miserable, but she'd grin cheerfully through her bouts of sickness and yell, "C'mon, waking early builds character! It's challenging!"

Diane felt the best thing you could do for yourself was to turn dreaded events into playful challenges. And while it was hard to appreciate this philosophy while I was struggling to keep my eyes open, she did eventually bring this message home to me through her views on grocery shopping.

As a single mother of four, Diane was responsible for keeping her household going, and one of the eternal challenges was keeping four growing kids fed. She did all of her family's grocery shopping, and rather than ducking this mundane task, she turned it into a game: She challenged herself to carry every bag in from the car at once. She would load herself up with bag after bag, strategically balancing the heavier and lighter items between both arms, and would stagger to the door, loaded down beyond belief. Somehow, despite the fact that she was shopping for five, she always managed to pull it off. And the pleasure she got over rising to the challenge she'd set made the whole trip worth it.

"Life is full of unpleasant tasks," Diane often said. "But put some fun into the drudgery. Make everything you do a challenge or a game, and always try to win. Never, ever, give up!"

To this day, I try to carry every grocery bag into the house at the same time. My old roommate thought I was crazy and complained that I'd drop or crush things. I just told her that the broken eggs and smashed bread can easily be recycled into French toast.

It is amazing how Di's out-of-the-ordinary challenges and her ways of coping with them have affected me over the years. I have grown to expect more of myself in both my personal and professional life. There are times when I am coaching and my players just don't get something or aren't working hard enough, and I want to give up and walk off the field. There are also times when I am running to get myself back in shape, and I feel I can't take another step. But Diane taught me to look at these obstacles as challenges, and when I do, I am usually successful.

"There is always a way to overcome them," Diane would say, "and it is not acceptable to just give up. Suck it up!" This infamous three-word saying of hers frequently echoes through my head. Once I have taken an extra step and realize that I have survived, taking the next one doesn't seem so hard.

Through Diane, I learned that any task, however menial, is worth doing right and doing completely. Take a job and tackle it head-on—make it fun, and get it done. It's a great feeling of accomplishment, and I'm sure that's what Diane wanted to impart to us.

EVERYONE
IS
INCLUDED

PATTI'S STORY

My sister Diane was devoted to everyone who crossed her path: family, friends, colleagues, and strangers. Each person was made to feel special, no matter who he or she was or what the occasion might have been. She was incredibly talented at welcoming individuals into the group; it was very important to her that no one ever be excluded.

These special people and loved ones were always included in Diane's beloved holidays. Later, her teams were included, whether we celebrated at her house or mine. She never seemed to sweat the details. I, on the other hand, often worried about how to clean and get everything prepared in time, how much of a mess might be made during a gathering, and how I was ever going to clean up afterward. When I mentioned these concerns to her, she simply shot back one of her favorite responses: "No problem." The only

---

PATTI GEPPI-GORSUCH *is one of Diane's beloved sisters who served as an honorary assistant coach at Loyola. She is a mother of two, John and Layne, as well as a surrogate mother to Diane's four children. Married for twenty-four years, she works two jobs and manages the household. She still finds time to enjoy walking, dancing, shopping, and spending time with family and friends.*

worry Diane ever expressed was, "I sure hope everyone has fun and enjoys themselves." It was much more important to her that we enjoy the company of family and friends than for everything to look and feel perfect.

Three years ago, Diane planned an Ocean City vacation with her four children, all of whom wanted to take a friend. Whereas most mothers would have refused, Diane, with her carefree spirit, zest for life, and good-time attitude, quickly agreed. On top of that, my children were going to Ocean City with friends, and they were going to be included in their aunt Diane's vacation as well.

Incidentally, this was a last-minute vacation decision booked during the peak of summer, and Diane could only find a one-bedroom rental with a sleep sofa. The place slept six, but Diane was determined to include everyone she had promised the trip to, so she made room for everyone—all fifteen.

"Find a pillow, a blanket, and a soft spot on the floor," she ordered, "because that's going to be your bed during this trip." You'd think that a house overrun with kids and no space to breathe would be a stressful spot for a working mother to wind down, but to Diane, it was the best because everyone was together and having fun.

Most kids that age wanted to get rid of their parents during beach vacations, but all these children and their friends included Diane in every one of their activities and fun. On trips to the Jolly Roger Amusement Park, Diane insisted on being first in line to test a carnival ride. If anyone debated that, she remarked loudly, "Hey, I brought you guys here, so I'm going first!" And far from being embarrassed by her behavior, the kids loved her silly persistence so much they begged for her to take them again and again.

A consummate athlete and coach, Di knew that life was a game. From lacrosse to Candy Land, Diane had game night at least once a week. Everyone and anyone could participate, including neighborhood kids and her players. What fun it was to hear the constant laughter when her house was filled with happy playing children. It didn't matter if Diane knew the kids or not, they were all welcome to participate. She often invited friends of her children who seldom had the opportunity to experience activities such as nature trips and hikes. "The more the merrier," she'd happily announce.

Even a simple trip to the zoo ended up consisting of a few carloads of rambunctious children. Diane never excluded anyone. If we were all looking at an animal, and a child couldn't see, she picked him up, talked to him, and made sure he was included. Half the time, other families—total strangers, mind you—joined us because it was so much fun.

Diane's all-inclusive philosophy even extended to decisions normally discussed only among her coaching staff. She requested input from other athletic department colleagues on game and coaching strategy. Now, this is not the norm for coaches, many of whom are very territorial about decisions regarding their team. Diane couldn't understand what benefit it would be to exclude anyone's opinion from consideration; she figured that everyone had an interesting and valuable perspective to offer, so it was important that these people be included.

I used to be uptight and very obsessive about everything I did, wanting things to look right rather than feel good. When I find myself feeling this way now, I remember how Diane taught me to "go with the flow, enjoy life to the fullest, find happiness within yourself, and always have fun with family, friends, work associates, and even strangers." Life is much more fun when you loosen up and let everyone in.

PERSEVERANCE, OR USING THE CAT BOWL

KERRI'S STORY

The most devastating, yet uplifting, experience of my life occurred during the holidays in December 2002. Diane got some very bad news at one of her doctor's appointments, which had become as regular as lacrosse practice by that time. On this visit, however, the doctor informed her that the cancerous tumor had returned to a place on the brain stem that was inoperable. According to the doctors, there were only a few options, and none of them was favorable. At this point, Diane was using a walker to help her get around at home and on the field, but she didn't let it slow down her life as a mother or a lacrosse coach.

When Diane received this difficult news, one of the first things she thought about was telling her players. By now, she had become a pretty high-profile story in the local press, and she worried that the media would leak the story. She did not want her team members to find out about her condition in

KERRI JOHNSON *is the new women's head lacrosse coach at Loyola. She served as an assistant and, later, associate head coach under Diane for six years. A three-time All-American and two-time first-team All-American selection and member of the U.S. national women's lacrosse team, Kerri also holds bachelor's and master's degrees in education.*

the paper or on television before she had time to tell them herself. It was holiday break time, and the players were scattered up and down the East Coast.

Diane asked me and the other assistant coaches to call all the players, who had been gone only about ten days, and ask them to come back for an emergency meeting. We also contacted parents, administrators, staff, mental health professionals from the counseling center, and the president of the college. Without hesitation, everyone returned to Loyola to take part in the meeting.

Eighty concerned people gathered in the Reading Room of the College Center prepared to listen, as always, to our coach. As Diane and her parents explained the grim diagnosis, many of these tough lacrosse players, including me, found their eyes filling up with tears. Diane continued her speech with a story, one of her favorite and most effective ways of relaying messages to us.

"Have trust in me," she began. "Have faith in God and persevere through all the challenges you come across in your day-to-day lives. If you do that, you can make it through anything. I'm going to need my friends and family around more now than ever before. Until now, I haven't needed twenty-four-hour help, and I've really enjoyed my independence. But I'm going to have to learn to rely on all of you as much as I can. Let me tell you a little story."

Diane explained to all of us that she usually carried her cell phone with her as she moved around the house with the aid of her walker. One day, however, she forgot to take her cell phone with her to the bathroom located on the other side of the house from her bedroom. As she was leaving the bathroom, she fell and was unable to lift herself back up: Her legs were too weak, and the walker was blocking the partially closed door. Frustrated and angry with herself, she was able to grab the walker and beat the door with it until she'd opened a space wide enough to slide through. She slowly crawled through one room and then another, becoming more exhausted by the minute.

Since Diane was on so many medications, she had to drink lots of fluids or her body could rapidly dehydrate. Recognizing her weakness and profuse perspiration as symptoms of dehydration, she became frightened. Suddenly, out of the corner of her eye, she spotted the cats' bowl of water as she pulled herself through the kitchen. Dragging herself a few more feet to the bowl, she hungrily lapped up the water and licked the bowl clean. Not the greatest drinking experience she'd ever had, but it was enough to temporarily refuel her. Three rooms and what seemed like hours later, she reached her cell phone and called her dad, who came to her house right away.

"If I can get through that," Diane said, "which was one of

the hardest experiences of my life, you gals can get through this season.

"I did what I had to do. The water was a little warm and dirty," Diane admitted, "but I happily drank it up. I did, however, make a mental note to keep the bowl and water a little fresher for the cats . . . and for me."

We all started laughing through our tears. It reminded us that Diane would do anything in her power to fight this awful disease. The moral of her story was to persevere, remain courageous, and try to find a little humor in adversity . . . even if you have to think like a cat!

Whenever I am faced with more obstacles than I think I can handle, I remember the cat bowl and Diane's amazing perseverance, and I find the strength to fight through them.

HONESTY AND LOVE

MONICA'S STORY

I met Diane for the first time in 1989 at the Baltimore-Washington International Airport train station. I had traveled from Newton Square, Pennsylvania, a town near Philadelphia, to Loyola College. Although it was my third visit to a Division I school as a lacrosse recruit, I was still scared out of my wits.

I had no idea what to expect from Loyola, or from Diane—I had no idea what she even looked like. But I would soon discover that even Diane's family and some of her oldest friends didn't always know what to expect from Diane. That was part of what made her so special—you never knew what she might say or do . . . or what she might wear.

When I stepped onto the platform that day, I saw a woman dressed entirely in Loyola's green and gray colors, holding hands with her children, four-year-old Michael and two-year-old Jessica. In typical Diane fashion, none of the

---

MONICA YEAKEL *served as Loyola's assistant women's lacrosse coach from 1994 to 1996, while teaching elementary school in Baltimore City. She became head women's lacrosse coach at the University of Maryland, Baltimore County, in 1997, and continues in that role today. She is married with one child, Luke.*

greens that she wore matched. Her outfit was a hodgepodge of different shades of gray and green—it was a pretty strange-looking getup, but I knew right away who she was. With all her other special qualities, her questionable fashion sense was not important.

I slid into Diane's car, and when she insisted that I sit up front, I immediately felt I had become a part of her family. There was an amazing comfort level that I had seldom felt before. I could be myself, and she even let me choose a radio station that I thought was better than the one she preferred. Diane was so unbelievably approachable—so "real." Maybe it was all those wacky shades of green.

The rest of the weekend was kind of a blur, but I do remember watching a night practice in the bitter February cold. Mesmerized, I stared as Diane coached and interacted with her players under the bright lights that illuminated their icy breath and reddened faces. They practiced drills over and over, and ran sprints forever. It was frigid out, but Diane made it look as if running in the frosty weather with your teammates was the best thing in the world. And the coaching—no matter what she yelled out, her players were ready and willing. There was a sense of trust and honesty that what Di was telling them to do was absolutely the right thing. They were in the zone, and it was only a practice! I remember thinking, *I could play here; I could belong here*, and I caught myself smiling, envisioning myself in a green-

and-gray uniform running across that chilly artificial turf.

One year later, there I was. I loved playing for Diane, but one of the hardest lessons I've ever endured was when I tore my anterior cruciate ligament, the connective tissue of my knee, at the beginning of my junior year. After reconstructive surgery and six arthroscopies, I couldn't play for more than a year. I felt removed from the team, as if I didn't really belong. I needed to get back on the field. My leg wasn't ready, but my mind was, so Diane let me play anyway. She knew that if I didn't get back to the field, I mentally might never make it back.

When I did finally play again, it didn't feel the same. My teammates kept telling me that I was just as good as before my knee injury. Somewhere deep inside, I knew this wasn't true. Although it felt great to be back on the team, it was so hard not to be the player I had been before.

Diane gave me the time I needed to realize this for myself before she gently but firmly told me I just wasn't fast enough to be out there that season. I had surmised it all along, and was really waiting—and wanting—for someone to tell me the truth. Although it was very difficult at the time, Diane was just being honest and open with me so that I could adapt and learn how to deal with my unfortunate situation. Without her honesty, I wouldn't have been able to grow and move forward.

Diane's method of honesty was never brutally frank, and

not at all hurtful. Unlike my sense of honesty, which was immature and abrasive back then, Diane's was laced with a semitough tenderness, full of love and hope. Her positive attitude and solid support helped me reevaluate my abilities, which allowed me to develop other skills to enhance my game. Instead of relying so much on my speed, I had to focus on my techniques on the field. That made me think more strategically about the game and learn to take other avenues, like cutting off lanes, running at angles, and anticipating where my opponents were headed. I got back on the field, and surprisingly to me, but not to Diane, I made All-American the following year. After college, I was selected to the U.S. women's team from 1994 to 1996.

Today, I am head coach at the University of Maryland, Baltimore County (UMBC), and my players know me best for my honesty and openness. Because of my experiences at Loyola, and mostly because of Diane, I strive to help others grow and learn, just as I did, with honesty and love.

When times were tough, Diane still took a chance on me and allowed me the opportunity to grow. She invited me to be a part of something so unique that I could never thank her enough. Now I take the tough love and integrity that she taught me and try to use it not just in my coaching, but also in my life.

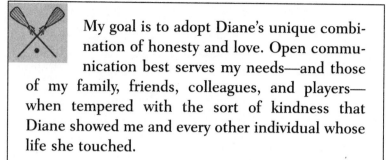

My goal is to adopt Diane's unique combination of honesty and love. Open communication best serves my needs—and those of my family, friends, colleagues, and players—when tempered with the sort of kindness that Diane showed me and every other individual whose life she touched.

OVERCOMING ADVERSITY

SUZANNE'S STORY

I came to Loyola's program from little-known North Harford High School in rural Maryland, which did not have a very good lacrosse team. Diane took a big chance when she brought me to Loyola, since she didn't know much about me. I wasn't a highly recruited player, and I'd done my share of stupid things in high school, one of which cost me my senior year's eligibility.

I think Diane must have viewed me as a challenge—she wanted to see if she could pull someone out of a bad situation and turn her around. I've heard that she used to say proudly of me, "This kid was a troublemaker who just wasn't always thinking right. I plucked her out of a high school environment where she had some problems, and at Loyola, she became a responsible athlete who completely buckled down and changed her attitude." Unfortunately, it didn't exactly happen overnight.

SUZANNE EYLER *graduated from Loyola in 2003 with a multitude of awards: three-time All-American; two-time first-team Colonial Athletic Association; Loyola College Leadership, Most Valuable Player, and Most Dedicated Player Awards; and Women's Lacrosse Coaches Association Attack Player of the Year. A psychology major, Suzanne is the assistant women's lacrosse coach at Towson University.*

In my freshman year at Loyola, I was having trouble academically. Because of social distractions, my grades were suffering and studying was almost nonexistent. I approached Diane, who sat me down and asked, "What can I do to help? Do you know about study hall?" I confessed that study hall was not helping me because I didn't know *how* to study.

Diane spoke with my academic supervisory service and helped them create a special study hall for athletes like me, who needed more quiet hours and lessons on studying techniques. They discovered that with me, it was figuring out what to study that was my biggest obstacle. Their plan for me worked. By my sophomore year, my grade point average had increased remarkably, and I never had academic problems at Loyola again. What's more, Diane had shown me that not only was my lack of study skills not an insurmountable problem, it was the key to my receiving the kind of extra help that would put me on top academically.

My academic woes weren't my only shortcoming. Unfortunately for me, my stature ensured that I would always "come up short" in the eyes of many; I'm only five-foot-one, and a lot of other college coaches felt that I was a good player, but just too small.

Diane, however, did not view my height as a disadvantage. She taught me that it was simply one of many adversities that I had to overcome as a player and a person. I had to get over the fact that I was short; there was nothing I could do about it.

"That's okay with me," Diane said. "It's okay to be little as long as you believe in yourself. It doesn't matter what other people think or say." In fact, she showed me that my height was disarming—no one expects the little one to be as fast and strong as I could be. With Diane's guidance, I overcame a number of adversities and had the opportunity to compete and play for her, and becoming a college All-American and Loyola Most Valuable Player under her tutelage was a major turning point in my life. Diane taught the importance of overcoming adversity throughout her career, always referring to her team as "Little Loyola, forever the underdog." I connected easily with that because I often felt like an underdog. Most schools looked down on Loyola, believing that they were going to tromp all over us because we had three thousand students and they had forty thousand. We never ever thought of ourselves as the "Big Dog" until the year we were finally ranked number one in America. Diane was right again—size didn't matter.

Watching Diane tackle and overcome her challenges made mine much more "doable." She viewed the roadblocks she faced as a woman, mother, coach, and individual as only speed bumps in her life. To overcome brain tumor operations, fighting for eight years just to stay alive for her family, team, and school, made my little setbacks seem quite manageable. She was truly inspirational because she not only "walked the walk and talked the talk," she did so much more. Diane taught us to believe in ourselves by being a living example for us, and I was so lucky to have the opportunity to be a part of her life.

Through Diane, I have learned that adversity is only as big as I choose to let it be. If I view it as an uphill battle, like a mammoth mountain, I'm never going to reach the top. But if I take adversity in stride, one day at a time, and maintain the constant belief that I *will* overcome it, then I will reach the top in the end.

NO STONE UNTURNED—THE THEMES OF THE SEASONS

KOURTNEY'S STORY

At the beginning of each spring season, Diane chose a theme for our team. Her themes were designed to jump-start and motivate the players. It was part of the buildup, something extra to top off the excitement, and she always presented the theme in the most dramatic and interesting way.

Every player received a T-shirt at the start of the season with the theme emblazoned on the back or front. We wore it to weight lifting, on away trips, around campus, and in the locker room—just like any other Loyola College–issued uniform. It was our own personal connection to each other as a team.

My sister, Krystin (an assistant coach at Loyola who also played there), and I sometimes debated which theme was our favorite. "How Would You Play Today if You Could Not Play Tomorrow?" came up frequently. Obviously, that theme was very inspirational since we never knew when it could be

---

KOURTNEY PORCELLA *was a High School Academic All-American soccer and lacrosse player from Bel Air, Maryland, who transferred to Loyola from Harford Community College. She is a team captain majoring in marketing.*

our last day of play. We busted our butts every day, knowing that it might be our final practice or game.

"You Control Your Own Destiny" was also a popular theme. Diane was sick of excuses, and fed up with the usual complaints: "I couldn't go to class because I was tired," or "I couldn't make it to practice on time," or "The refs called a bad game," or "The weather was bad."

"Just forget all that!" retorted Diane. "Too many excuses. You need to take personal responsibility and control your own destiny. You can't control the weather outside, you can't control what officials are going to be like during a game, and you can't control where the ball is going to bounce. But you can control the way you react, how hard you work, and your attitude. It's important that you don't get wrapped up in excuses."

I came to realize that there really are many things we *do* have control over. Diane did not have control over her brain tumor, but she did have control over how she reacted to it, her attitude toward it, and how she decided to live her life from that point on.

Those themes were great, but my favorite theme was "No Stone Unturned." Diane came up with that after she told us that she was sick with another tumor. She said, "I don't want any regrets this season. I am going to do everything I can to make us win, and you guys are going to do everything you can to make us win. We'll leave no stone unturned. Every day at practice, every day you get together as a team, and every day you are out there alone, you have to do everything in your power to make sure you are the most prepared you can be. When you walk off this field in May thinking that you did everything you possibly could to be the best that you could be, then you've left no stone unturned."

"No Stone Unturned" also meant to practice full tilt. "Don't do anything halfheartedly," stressed Diane. "If you're going to do something, make the effort to do it right. Go all out and give me all you have." If we were lagging at practice or down at halftime in a game, she would write NO STONE UNTURNED in large letters on the chalkboard to get us pumped up.

These themes and their lessons carried far beyond lacrosse. Diane encouraged us to work as hard as we could with our academics, family life, relationships, present jobs, and future careers. The shirts were not designed just to get us through hours of practice and games. Diane made sure that the lessons we learned in lacrosse could be applied for a lifetime.

When I approach a difficult situation now in school, relationships, or life, I try to create a theme that helps me deal with it. This seemingly gimmicky tool really helps me to get to the heart of any matter, stay true to myself, and follow the right path in whatever I do.

WARM AND FUZZY MOMENTS

TARA'S STORY

After a rough loss or a few days of intense practices when we were feeling down, Diane would lead the team through a routine she called "warm and fuzzy moments." She would take out a stuffed animal or even a roll of toilet paper and say, "All right, Tara, you take this and throw it to another player. But before you do that, you have to say something nice about her." It didn't have to be lacrosse-related. It could be any reason why that person was special to you or the team. The idea was to give the person a warm and fuzzy feeling, and it proved to be very contagious.

We could pass it to anyone we chose, and eventually everyone caught whatever we were passing around. Diane encouraged us to choose people who weren't our best friends or roommates. I usually picked someone I either didn't know very well or had a small issue with, and I always found something nice to say about this girl, whether it was

Tara Singleton *is a senior midfielder at Loyola and a team captain. She is a member of the U.S. Developmental Lacrosse Team. Tara is majoring in elementary education.*

"thanks for helping me prepare for that math test" or "you had an amazing assist in that last drill." I found that it really did feel good.

Since each person brought different qualities to the team, and the warm and fuzzy moments showed that everyone was important, we learned what we truly meant to one another. I never would have known that I had really helped someone out or that I was special to someone without this game, and I came to look forward to the times when we played it.

As time and tradition progressed, warm and fuzzy moments evolved into instances or situations that were magical and emotional. I have three favorites.

Diane called us inside in the middle of practice one day and said, "I have something I want you to listen to. I had my kids make this special CD for me, with a bunch of my favorite songs."

Before playing each song, she would comment, sort of like a disc jockey, and dedicate the songs to her children. "This is what Shannon and I sing every day before we go to school," or "This song is mine and Melissa's."

Most of the tunes were disco-like, and she told us to relax and "boogie on down." She played about five songs for us before changing the upbeat mood with one called "There Are Angels Among Us." It was the first time I had ever heard it, and Di sang along. We cried and held hands as she played the song she obviously felt very strongly about. She smiled, and we could see that she was happy. Coach Diane wanted to share this with us, and let us in on another intimate aspect of her life—a very warm and fuzzy moment.

Another emotional moment took place during our miracle 2003 season. The school rented a handicapped-accessible van for Diane so she could travel to the games in her wheelchair. It could accommodate only seven players, and we drew names out of a hat to see who'd receive the honor of riding with the coach. The other players followed in Loyola's regular vans.

"Pops," her dad, drove the special plain white van. Before we picked up Diane, we decorated it with streamers, balloons, ribbons, and two big signs. One said HONK TWICE FOR DI, and the other over the windshield said THE DI MOBILE. As Pops brought Diane out of her house, she saw the van and started crying. She was so happy, and we were even happier. Another very special moment.

My other favorite warm and fuzzy moment took place during fall practice. Once a week, and we never knew which day, Diane would cancel half or all of practice for a team breakfast. One particular time she gave us a list of questions to answer, such as describing our greatest fear, our greatest achievement, and our greatest dream. One by one we discussed our answers.

Diane went last, because she had a hard time figuring out her greatest fear; she really wasn't afraid of anything. All her answers dealt with her family and her team, and the pride that they made her feel. And then she let us in on her greatest fear. It was her fear of her children being scared about losing their mother. It was not about her own fear of dying, but about the kids' fear of her dying. We had never heard her express this concern, since it was before we found out that her brain tumor was terminal. That was a very emotional moment.

The week before Diane passed away, we went to her house to visit. She was on morphine and was very tired, sleeping for long periods of time. We were sitting around outside of her room telling stories when all of a sudden we heard, "Hello! I hear you guys. Get in here. Let's have a warm and fuzzy moment."

Diane proceeded to tell funny and touching stories about each of us. Because we were by her side, she became awake and alive. She hadn't spoken for sixteen hours, but after hearing the voices of her thirty-five extra kids, as she called us, Diane reemerged.

We were so lucky to be with her and her family during those final weeks. In a way, we were her family, too. She made us such a big part of her life, and was such an unselfish and wonderful person. It reinforced how much we meant to her, and she to us.

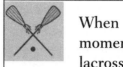 When I think back, those warm and fuzzy moments really had nothing to do with lacrosse. They were about being there for one another. And the lesson I learned was that there is more to life than winning, and more to winning than the final score. There are warm and fuzzy moments all around us—we just need to take the time to stop and point them out to each other and to ourselves.

······ ❖ ······

PLAYING
FOR
RESPECT

JANINE'S STORY

······ ❖ ······

One of the most vivid memories I have of Diane Marie Geppi-Aikens took place in the spring of 1990. I graduated in 1989 after playing lacrosse and field hockey at Loyola College, and Diane coached me in my senior year. She asked me to stay on board as an assistant coach after graduation, and I was thrilled at the opportunity. We had a hugely successful lacrosse season that year and were set to play in the semifinals of the NCAA tournament, which was quite a triumph for little Loyola College at the time. As we took the field against the powerful University of Maryland, I could tell that our team was a little nervous, and Diane sensed it as well. We did our best to convince our players

---

JANINE TUCKER *recently completed her tenth season as the head women's lacrosse coach at Johns Hopkins University. A 1989 graduate of Loyola College, Tucker, who has compiled a 122-45 (.731) overall mark, is the winningest coach in school history. Recently she cowrote a book with Maryalice Yakutchik titled* The Baffled Parent's Guide to Coaching Girls' Lacrosse. *Janine also set up a Web site for Diane at www.caringbridge.org/md/aikens. In January 2003, both Janine and her husband, John, were inducted into the Greater Baltimore Chapter of the U.S. Lacrosse Hall of Fame. The Tuckers have two sons, Ryan and Devin.*

that they deserved to be there, and sent them on their way to take on the "Terps."

Shockingly, halfway through the first half we were losing 7–1. We weren't used to being down by that much, that quickly, and Diane and I could see the team's confidence ebbing with every minute. Being a young novice coach, I was getting frustrated myself and feeling sorry for the girls as they struggled to keep the game within reach. At halftime, the score was Maryland 8 . . . Loyola 1. Not happy times.

We were clearly outmatched. The Terps were bigger, stronger, faster, and better skilled than our Greyhounds, and I was prepared for Diane to give a consoling halftime speech. I figured she would let the team know we were proud of them for trying their best, for hanging in there with the adjustments we had made, and for giving it their best shot no matter what happened or what would happen in the next half. Boy, was I wrong.

Before the team had a chance to sit down in the locker room, clipboards and chairs started flying, and Diane's screams could be heard halfway across the building.

"What's the matter with you guys?" Diane demanded. "How dare you hang your heads! Do you think this game is over? Are you just going to stop playing and feel sorry for yourselves because we're losing by a few goals? Let me tell you something . . . we may be outmatched, but not only do you play to win . . . you play for *respect*. I don't care if we

go out there and Maryland scores five more quick goals . . .
you will *not* hang your heads . . . you will *not* walk . . . you
will *not* give up . . . you will *never* give up as long as you are
playing for me!

"You will play for the reputation of this school, your personal reputations, the reputations of your teammates, and
for *respect!* Do you hear me? You want that Maryland team
to walk off that field, no matter what the final score,
respecting you for your fight and determination. Don't you
dare waste my time by not giving me a thousand percent no
matter what the outcome of the game. You are *not* giving me
enough right now . . . not even close! Do you understand
me?"

Well, we were all in such shock that only a muffled "yes"
came out of the girls' mouths . . . mine included.

"*What?*" Diane bellowed. "I asked you if you understand
what I am saying to you! Answer me with some conviction!"

"*Yes!*" screamed the team with everything they had in
them.

It gave me chills then and it gives me chills to this day
thinking about their reaction. Diane wasn't finished
speaking, but the captains took over. They started encouraging their teammates, banging on the lockers, banging their
sticks, and kicking the chairs. The team went into a frenzy
right there in front of us. We looked at each other and realized there was nothing more to be said. The girls knew they

were capable of performing better on the field, and they were prepared to do just that in the second half . . . and did they ever!

The Greyhounds came out with a newfound confidence and huddled together before taking the field. They vowed to give us a thousand percent no matter what the outcome of the game, and as they raised their sticks high in the air, they screamed *"Respect"* at the top of their lungs. The Terps took one look and knew they were in for a battle. And what a battle it was. Diane and I proudly watched as our players fought for every loose ball, shot with everything they had in them, and came up big on the defensive end of the field. When it was all said and done, Loyola won the second half 4–2, but it wasn't enough to defeat the Terps, who'd had that commanding 8–1 lead in the first half. But the Greyhounds didn't care. They may have lost the game 10–5, but what they remembered was winning that second half in more ways than one.

It was then that I knew how special a coach Diane was, because our girls were celebrating as if they had just won the game. It was priceless. Diane had made a profound impact on that team that carried over into the next year, and the next year, and the next.

When I look back on that game, it always brings a smile to my face. No, we didn't win that particular contest, but we won in so many other ways. We learned about playing for respect despite the odds. The phrase *playing for respect* rings in my ears in many situations that I have faced in life. What does it mean to me? It means performing in such a way, behaving in such a way, that no matter what the outcome, my opponent and those observing can't help but develop a deep respect for me. It means never giving up and having so much pride and self-confidence in who I am that I never hang my head, never allow *me* to beat myself.

> Thanks to Diane, I've learned to "play for respect" in every aspect of my life, always seeking to fight with a higher purpose, not just to win the game, but to establish myself as a person . . . because the fights develop character, strengthen dignity, reveal integrity, and make me live more fully.

TENACITY, OR HOW TO TURN A SUBURBAN INTO A SNOWPLOW

STEPHANIE'S STORY

If tenacity revealed is the mark of a triumphant spirit, Diane may have been the most triumphant spirit ever to have lived. Diane's tenacity was legendary. After her first surgery, her mother pleaded with the surgeon to not let her go on the lacrosse field right away. But the doctor wouldn't make the call, explaining, "That's Diane's decision to make."

So here was Diane, with staples in her head, insisting to her parents, "I have to go to the college to see my girls." Knowing her illness hadn't dampened her will, her dad drove her there himself rather than fight a losing battle over allowing her to go. Soon after, she told them, "I need to go on a recruiting trip," so her dad drove her to New Jersey. And the day after that, Diane and her father traveled to Pennsylvania. Most of the recruits and their parents were so impressed with Diane's drive that they decided that Loyola

---

STEPHANIE ANNE SWEET, *aka "Sweethead," played at Loyola from 1996 to 2000. A team captain in 1999 and 2000, she was the recipient of the Loyola College Athletic Department Leadership Award. Sweet worked as an assistant coach and physical education professor at Duke University from 2000 to 2003. She is currently living in California, completing a master's degree in biomechanics/kinesiology. She works as an ocean lifeguard during the summer.*

College was the best place to attend, and it ended up being one of her best recruiting trips ever.

A couple of years later, on a freezing February day, a significant amount of snow and ice had accumulated on the game field. Since our field was made of artificial turf, we figured it would be easy for us to clear it and move forward with practice, with very little time wasted. But in a span of only four days, it snowed some more, then iced over, then snowed again. Finally, the sun came out, but the warmth only packed the snow tighter together.

Our team began to shovel, splitting the field with the men's lacrosse players. Progress was very slow, and what we could not shovel right away turned into heavier snow and harder sheets of ice. In some areas of the turf, the smashed white powder was waist-high. We organized shoveling shifts between classes, hoping that there would be enough space on the field when we finished to hold some form of outdoor practice. As if this weren't bad enough, our first home game was rapidly approaching—it was scheduled in less than a week.

A few days of indoor practices passed by slowly. There was only so much situational play that could be done in a gym before both coaches and players started getting antsy. On the sixth day, we attempted to shovel the field again without much success. This time, though, Diane had an idea. Insisting that "practice must go on!" she disappeared for five minutes without saying a word.

Suddenly, the gates to Curley Field opened, and a blue Suburban appeared on the edge of the turf, like the beginning of a Chevy commercial. We heard Diane shift her truck into four-wheel drive and rev the engine. Snowdrifts were higher than the vehicle's tires. The "Like a Rock" musical jingle played loudly in my head as our coach forcefully attacked each of the stubborn snow and ice chunks with her "family car."

With shovels in our hands, clothed only in our Loyola practice gear, we stood motionless for a moment in amazement, deciding whether it was even safe to be standing there watching. A second later, laughter echoed across the field, and everyone started feeling excited over the possibility of an outdoor practice.

Crack, squeak, crack, squeak . . . Over the ice chunks the determined Suburban's shocks crunched. Diane stuck her head out the window, yelling one of her favorite expressions, "Yee-hah!" as if she were riding a bucking bronco. Before long, we noticed that parts of Di's truck were starting to loosen. We tried to give her demonstrative signals, like jumping up and down, waving our arms, pointing and laughing, holding our heads in our hands, and mouthing, "Oh, man!"

Freshmen who didn't know Diane very well were shell-shocked. They had never seen her act out before. As the cheering grew louder, Diane continued to ram every snow pile around the field. Faculty began poking their heads out of their office windows in amazement. The truck barreled on. When she could no longer move, she would quickly back up, grinding the gears, and lurch forward again.

For another half hour, Diane continued to plow, happily singing along with a tune on the radio. She opened her window and gleefully yelled, "Practice will go on!" Sure enough, her undercarriage broke loose and was noisily dragging on the field. But *no* . . . she wasn't stopping. There was still more ice to be broken up to create enough field on which to practice. Soon after that, she lost the bumper, and then the side mirror vibrated completely off and fell to the ground. Diane didn't seem to notice and probably didn't really care, so she never looked back. When she finally jumped out of the Suburban, everyone loudly applauded.

Practice *was* held on Curley Field that day, and it will forever be remembered as the day Di tested the limits of her truck. For a coach who was willing to put as much fire and energy into clearing part of a field for her players, it was only natural for us to want to give it back.

Diane was a true leader—and one who led by example. From this exceptional woman I learned that if a decision has to be made, make it with confidence and conviction, and stick to it. Whether the decision was right or wrong is often relative, but the rewards of such tenacious behavior are always plentiful.

······ ❖ ······

PREPARATION
AND
VISUALIZATION

MARIANNE'S STORY

······ ❖ ······

As a coach, Diane believed you could never be too prepared. "Preparation teaches you how to roll with the punches," she said, meaning that if we were totally mentally prepared, when the unexpected arose, we would be ready.

This philosophy meant that we ran drills thousands of times to be sure our skills would be there when we needed them; that we scrimmaged in endless combinations until every play felt like second nature.

From bad calls by officials, to showing up late for a game, to inclement weather, we would practice it. In thunderstorms or blizzards, we would still practice. "You can't predict or control Mother Nature. We have to be able to play in undesirable conditions, too, and we'll be used to it and ready for it," Diane would explain. "Our opponents won't."

MARIANNE GIOFFRE *graduated in 2003 and is pursuing a master's degree in school counseling. She is currently a volunteer coach at Loyola College. A first-team All-American in 2003, Marianne was on the NCAA All-Tournament team last year. She majored in advertising and marketing, and is from Annapolis, Maryland.*

But she didn't want us just to prepare for the normal contingencies; Diane came up with the craziest, most unorthodox situations. "Suppose you find yourself rolling on the ground with the ball in your stick," she would say, "and three people are chopping at you with their sticks?" Before we could answer, she would have us on the ground practicing the scenario. It might have seemed silly—and believe me, we did our share of laughing on the ground, warding off attacks from above—but it helped to have experience with the unexpected.

And it wasn't only the big-picture concepts she prepared us for—minute details mattered just as much to her. For example, if we were used to sitting on the same bench all season, she would prepare us for the possibility that we might be sitting on the opposite side of the field when we went to the NCAA tournament. We'd practice sitting on the other bench so that nothing could throw us when the big event came along.

Of course, visualization was also a key factor. Before every game, Diane instructed us to go to our rooms and mentally prepare before falling asleep. "While you are lying in bed, think of a big thing and a little thing. Think about blocking a shot or stopping a one-on-one situation. Think about scoring a goal and picking up a ground ball. If there is one minute left in the game and we are up by one or down by one, you should know what you are going to do."

In other words, Diane wanted us to be calm and panic-free. I watched so much game film of my opponents that I knew what they were going to do before they did it. "If you are prepared, you will win," was a saying Diane repeated over and over.

The day before a big game, Diane would begin practice by moving the players to the sidelines and have Sara, who had a beautiful voice, sing the national anthem. We prepared as if it were the actual game so that none of us would have the jitters or feel nervous. We liked it that Diane would help prepare us this way, closing our eyes and listening to Sara's words. Even if something negative occurred before, during, or after the game, we were always prepared. We weren't even unprepared for Diane's death, because when she knew she was going to die, she called us together to let us know, and she helped us understand that we could handle losing her, just as we could handle any of the other curves life threw us. It was hard, but the preparation she drilled into each and every one of us truly did make this tragic event more bearable.

Looking back, I realize that what Diane taught us through preparation and visualization was about being a responsible adult. If we picture all the things that could go wrong in, say, arriving on time for work, or picking up our kids after school, we can better handle the inevitable situations that pop up, and can take it in stride calmly and coolly, just as Diane would have wished.

HONOR THY PARENTS

RACHEL'S STORY

When I left home to attend Loyola, it was such a relief to be away from my parents and their nagging questions. I often had a bad attitude in their presence, and rarely told them anything about my life. Through Diane's wise words and living examples, however, I grew to understand that my parents were the two most important people in my life.

Family was first and foremost to Diane, and this included her team, whom she lovingly referred to as her "second family." Her father was present at every single game she ever played in or coached. He wasn't as vocal as her mom, though, who yelled, cheered, even waved a set of pom-poms. Her mom also loved to chat with the parents at tailgate parties and games. Like Diane, she had a way of making everyone feel good.

Diane always showed her parents tremendous respect, generously bestowing hugs and kisses every time she saw them. If she was coaching and needed their help, she

RACHEL SHUCK *is from Annapolis, Maryland, and is a senior at Loyola with two seasons of lacrosse eligibility remaining. In 2003, she made All-American, and in 2004 Rachel is a team captain.*

treated them just as she would her other assistant coaches. They were basically included in everything, and even rode on the bus with us to every game.

Diane's respect for her mom and dad quickly rubbed off on us. She would frequently ask questions about our families, and had dedicated all their names, including those of our siblings, to memory—an amazing feat. When she gave us her "priorities speech," parents were always first on the list.

Diane wanted us to share all the ups and downs of our lives with our moms and dads. When she proudly told us stories about her children, who would come to her first with all their problems, it made us long to have that relationship with our own parents. She was so pleased that her kids shared their issues, however bad, with their mom. The respect and love that the children had for Diane were obvious, and Diane's respect for them was unquestionable.

I got into trouble once at Loyola for going to a bar while I was underage. I couldn't imagine confessing to my parents, so the first person I went to with this problem was Diane. I trusted her, and I knew she understood me. "What should I do?" I asked.

"Call home and tell your parents immediately," she quickly responded. "They'll understand. You're young . . . it happens."

So I did just that. They were angry, but appreciated that they heard the bad news first from me and not secondhand from the school. At the end of the conversation, my mom asked, "Did you tell the coach?"

"Actually," I said, "I told Diane about it first."

Diane often stressed that parents were number one during her after-game locker room speeches, in front of her players, alumni, and the players' parents. "Thank your parents for supporting you," she ordered, "and go over right now and hug and kiss them. And don't forget to tell them how much you love them!"

Up until a week before Diane took a turn for the worse, my teammates and I would visit her at her house to cheer her up. Although not feeling well, she still made it a point to ask about our moms and dads and share stories about her parents and children.

"Call them," Diane ordered as we were leaving, something she reminded us to do almost from the moment we met her. "And not just when you want something. Call them because you love them and you want to share your experiences with them. You know, you *are* here because of your parents."

Before meeting Diane, I took my parents for granted a bit, but her example taught me that the more room I make in my life for my parents, the more they enhance my life.

NEVER
GROW UP

PORCH'S STORY

During my first year of coaching with Diane, we traveled to Brown University for a game. The night before the game, we joined the three Brown lacrosse coaches, all good friends, for a beer at the hotel bar. Diane ordered two bottles of Miller Lite and turned to me with an impish smile on her face.

"Porch, how about a contest?" she dared. "You're young and hip and right out of college, and I'll bet you think you can drink some beers. But let me show you how it's done."

Diane took one of the beer bottles and placed it upright on top of her head. Then, in one swift motion, without moving her head, she grabbed the bottle, flipped it over, and drank the whole beer without spilling a drop. And that was just the test run to show me how it was done.

KRYSTIN "PORCH" PORCELLA *attended Loyola College from 1994 to 1998. She played four years of soccer and four years of lacrosse, and was selected two-time All-American and two-time U.S. team member. After graduating, she took an assistant coaching job in women's lacrosse at Virginia Tech in Blacksburg, Virginia, for two years. In 2000, she returned to Loyola to coach under Diane.*

Diane ordered a beer for me and picked up her remaining bottle. "One, two, three, let's go!" she ordered, and we proceeded with the contest. She was great, never spilling a drop. I, of course, spilled the beer all over the front of my shirt and jeans, leaving a large puddle of foam on the floor.

"Okay," said Diane, "let's go. We've got a big game tomorrow. No more beer."

"But I didn't drink any," I pleaded.

"Too bad," she said, laughing. "Maybe we'll compete again another time."

"Very funny," I deadpanned. "And *very* juvenile!"

Now, I didn't think this verbal slap was a winner, but it was the best I could do off the top of my head. But as soon as I'd uttered the word *juvenile,* a huge smile broke across Diane's face. You see, to her, telling folks they were acting immature was the biggest compliment you could give. As Diane walked toward the exit, she turned and responded, "Never grow up, Porch, that's the secret." Then, without missing a beat, she added, "And clean yourself up. You look like a slob!"

I learned a great lesson by losing that childish contest to Diane: You can still have fun while being responsible and working hard. Working hard is balanced out by relaxing when you're not. It's okay to have fun!

Diane felt she had a better chance of making an impact on someone through humor and fun than tedious lecturing.

Sure, there were times to get serious, but she strove to make a humorous impression whenever possible. My very first encounter with Diane was at our initial team meeting in the fall of my freshman year. She stood in front of us and introduced herself, before abruptly climbing on top of the table to begin her speech. To our surprise, she then jumped on a nearby chair as she continued to speak. Before we knew it, she had leaped on top of a podium under a television, strategically squishing herself between the two. We were suppressing our laughter as Diane was talking and bouncing around the room with tons of energy and excitement, getting us psyched for the coming year.

It was a different approach and almost ridiculous, but we naturally responded to it because it was lively and childlike. We learned that it was okay to show enthusiasm and express our true emotions, however juvenile, through demonstrative physical behavior. And we learned that some rules were meant to be broken.

Another way Diane demonstrated her reverence for acting young was through her style of dress. Fashion was clearly not one of Diane's strengths. Actually, she had no sense of fashion at all, and she knew it. But she was okay with that, and it was all right for her family and us to tell her what to wear, or to point out that something didn't match— which was very frequently.

Each year, Diane would appoint one or two players as her

fashion police to tell her if her clothes didn't match. Even as an adolescent, she never thought fashion mattered. To her, there was no need for things to match or be in style. They were just clothes. It was restricting and too adultlike, a grown-up thing.

Stories abound about Diane's unique sense of style. Especially memorable were her pink sweatpants. Not a light, conservative pink; but a deep, bright, fluorescent pink. She wore them for years to practice because they were her "favorite, most comfortable sweatpants." At last, the team had them banned from the field for being so ludicrous and distracting. After many attempts, we finally convinced Diane to throw her beloved sweats away, or so we believed. Weeks later, we spied them under another pair of sweats.

On the field one day, Diane confidently strutted onto the turf with cowboy boots, a fringed cowboy top, and matching fringed pants—a bold statement that is another classic memory. It was probably the only matching outfit she ever wore. It looked absolutely ridiculous, but we admired her courage for wearing it.

I think that Diane looked upon fashion as too strict and too organized, and not important enough to be a part of her life. It reminded me of the magnet on her refrigerator that read "A clean house is a sign of a wasted life . . ." And

Diane definitely didn't have a clean house, car, or office. There were piles of papers scattered about, toys, pictures painted by her kids, things plastered all over the walls, and bikes littering the yard and porch; but there was love everywhere.

One day, a couple of years ago, an almost-forty-year-old Diane came to work wearing her thirteen-year-old daughter Jessica's clothes. Jessica had picked out the outfit, and without hesitation, Diane, who amazingly could still wear children's clothes, proudly wore it. She wore a low-rise denim miniskirt with a big, loose-fitting chain-link belt, Reebok street-wear white sneakers with little pink anklet socks, and a white fitted T-shirt. She also accessorized with large hoop earrings and matching silver bracelets. Others may have been embarrassed to parade around wearing their children's clothing, but not Diane—she swaggered around with the air of someone who knew she looked great.

After an early-morning meeting with Diane, one of the players quickly spread the news of the coach's latest fashion faux pas. Nearly every player and assistant coach on the team stopped by her office to see her attire. It was a truly awesome sight. Later, when I saw Diane, she was smiling. I shook my head at her outfit, and she winked and said, "Porchy, never grow up."

Too many people go through life trying to maintain strict control, wearing poker faces and hiding their true emotions. But not Diane. Her zest for life was contagious, and like anyone who knew her, I learned an important lesson from Diane: Life is too short to skip the fun. Keeping yourself young and appreciating laughter is the best life plan.

TURN NEGATIVES INTO POSITIVES

BETSY'S STORY

O f all the unique qualities that Diane possessed, the one I think defined her was her positive attitude. When she was pregnant with her fourth child, Shannon, the doctors suspected that the baby might be born with Down syndrome.

Diane never expressed any doubts about giving birth to a Down baby. Instead of lamenting this possibility or referring to the expected child as disabled or cursed, she felt that she had been blessed. She set about finding out as much information as she could about parenting a Down syndrome child, and since she knew I had an aunt who had Down, she came to me with a few pragmatic questions.

BETSY ECONOMOU *was the 1990 Maryland High School Athlete of the Year and was selected to the All-Metro soccer, basketball, and lacrosse teams. She played all three of these sports at Loyola from 1990 to 1995, a rarity in Division I collegiate athletics. She made the All-American lacrosse team in 1995, and was the all-time leading scorer in soccer. Betsy received an MBA in marketing from Loyola, served as Loyola's assistant soccer coach, and later was the head lacrosse coach at Greenwich High School in Connecticut. She founded Impact Lacrosse, the premier girls' lacrosse development program in the country.*

"How did your family deal with Annie?" asked Diane.

"It was difficult and challenging," I said, "especially for the primary caregivers. But she was a blessing in our lives, who brought laughter to us all."

"And what was her functioning level?" Diane continued.

"Down babies born in 1963 were basically counted out. Aunt Annie defied everything the doctors said, one of which was that she would never function in society. She graduated from high school, and we think it was because the family treated her as if she were normal."

Finally, Diane asked a question that concerned her three other children. "How did Annie interact with her seven siblings?"

"They all got along great," I boasted.

"That's just what I wanted to hear," she said, beaming.

She was preparing herself, but she never showed any remorse or sadness. "I'm going to have a special child," she bragged. "God must feel I'm just the kind of mother to handle it."

Diane tackled every problem in her life head-on, never running away or hiding. Here she was, with three kids and the number-two–ranked team in the United States, with so much on her plate that it would be understandable—even expected—for her to worry over how she would cope. Instead, she accepted this as a challenge she could easily handle; Diane figured God wouldn't throw her any curveballs she couldn't catch. To witness such a positive outlook in a situation that could cast such dark shadows on many other people's lives was life altering for me. Shannon was ultimately born without Down syndrome, but there would be plenty of other challenges ahead for Diane.

When Diane first discovered she needed surgery for her cancer, her positive outlook made her try hard to convince us not to take her illness seriously. We were quite upset and distraught, and it was a very traumatic time for all of us. But more than anything, Diane wanted us to be lighthearted and not to worry. That was Diane . . . always thinking of everyone else first.

"Look, girls," she said, "if I were all grown up and real mature, this surgery could have made me clinically depressed, and might have even landed me in a rubber room. But thankfully, I've never grown up, and I'm still able to find the positives in this very negative predicament."

"How's that?" I asked, skeptical, but my curiosity piqued.

Diane quickly retrieved her driver's license, so excited to show us that she spilled the contents of her purse all over the floor. Since she was experiencing mild seizures that could occur at any time, the Maryland Motor Vehicle Administration had listed her symptoms on the back of her license.

"Look at this," she said proudly. "Now if I ever get pulled over for drinking, I won't have to worry about it. I'll be able to whip out my license and say, 'I'm having a seizure, Officer!' Then I'll be off the hook, scot-free." She acted so excited that we were almost feeling jealous. Of course, we knew how very opposed Diane was to drinking and driving, and how she always insisted on designated drivers. She would never *need* this excuse; it was simply her way of looking on the bright side of things.

Diane was so proud of her teams at Loyola, especially since we weren't a big-time Division I school with a major football program. We didn't have the greatest facilities, and we couldn't even sign up our athletes for special "athlete" classes the way the bigger schools could. With all these limitations, we still managed to compete fiercely and upset many schools that had more tools with which to help their athletes. To Diane, that made little Loyola all the more special.

When I last visited Di, she told me that she wasn't sure whether she had days, months, or years to live. There was no negativity, regret, or blame in her voice. Instead, she said she felt blessed to know what her future held. It gave her the opportunity to prepare, something most people didn't have. She could kiss her children ten times a day and tell them how much she loved them. She could tell her parents that they meant the world to her. She could hug the members of her team, and tell them how proud she was of their accomplishments. And she could call on a few of her close friends, including me, to help prepare and deliver her eulogies.

She *would,* however, fight to think, act, and feel as positive as she could every single day. And she *would* live each moment to the fullest for as long as she had on this great earth. And she would be positive till the end.

Diane's ability to turn negatives into positives is my guiding principle; because of her cheerful good spirits, I join all who knew her in looking on the bright side in any difficult situation, and I know I live life more fully because of it.

KNOW YOUR ROLE—THE VALUE OF TEAMWORK

KIM'S STORY

Diane was a recruiting whiz, so the Loyola team was always chock-full of amazing talent. She was also, however, completely committed to the belief that a good team is made up of more than just outstanding players, and she prided herself on putting together teams filled with players who knew their roles. Good students, inspirational team cheerleaders, or players who had atypical styles of play that complemented the skills of others were assets to the team as well. There were no prejudices in Diane's life or in her coaching of the game of lacrosse.

Diane made everyone on the team feel special with her genuinely unbiased attitude. Many found it hard to believe that she never favored the better players, actually speaking more to the average players on the bench. She made sure that they, too, felt confident and comfortable. In fact, she loved it when someone with lesser natural ability showed up

---

KIM LAWTON *is the senior goalie for the Greyhounds. In 2003, she enjoyed the lowest goals-against average in Division I women's lacrosse. An elementary education major, she made dean's list in her sophomore year.*

one of the team phenoms, and would always call attention to these minor victories for the underdog, crowing, "You may outrun her, but look how fast she *made* you run!"

How good someone was as a player mattered little to Diane, as long as she knew she was there to do a job and did it. Diane believed that the girls who weren't necessarily the greatest players still brought to the team what many others couldn't. Kate Plantholt, who had a bad back and couldn't play, was valued for delivering a different team prayer before every game. "There's more than one way to be a good player," Diane sympathized. There were actually many players whose off-field contributions enhanced the on-field action in subtle, but important, ways. Sara Shoaf, who sang "The Star-Spangled Banner" before each home game or in preparation for a key contest, had an amazingly powerful voice, and Diane correctly predicted that listening to this gorgeous sound bursting forth from one of our teammates was just what we needed to get psyched up to play. "Everyone has a special role in this game, and success comes from off-field players as well as on-field players."

Diane supported this girl's role, along with that of the player who delivered a different inspirational team prayer before every game. To the rest of the team and to these players themselves, she insisted that their contributions were just as vital as those of a high scorer or an aggressive defender. And when Diane lost the use of her left arm and couldn't turn the pages of a scouting report or travel itinerary, she turned to freshman defender Kristen McKay and told her she would be lost without her help in flipping the pages.

As a result of all the remarkable teamwork, the Greyhounds were more than just successful. They were unique. There were teams with the best talent around who turned out to be just mediocre because they did not play as a team. Often, talented individual players refused to accept lesser roles for the good of the group, or friction between some of the girls resulted in a lack of camaraderie and teamwork.

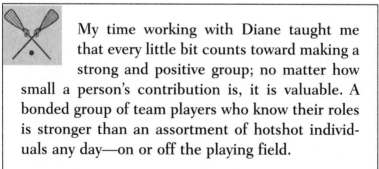

My time working with Diane taught me that every little bit counts toward making a strong and positive group; no matter how small a person's contribution is, it is valuable. A bonded group of team players who know their roles is stronger than an assortment of hotshot individuals any day—on or off the playing field.

INTENSITY

ANDY'S STORY

I distinctly remember the very first occasion when I saw Diane in 1983. A senior in high school at the time, I was visiting Loyola to take my placement test and watch my future team battle the Dukes of James Madison. There, in the goal for Loyola, was a diminutive fireball. Diane was the smallest goalie I had ever seen, yet the most aggressive, the most athletic, and by far the quickest. But even more impressive was her incredible intensity. It could be seen in the way she deftly moved, and heard in the way she confidently voiced directives to all the players. She was fully engaged in the game for every single minute that she played, never letting her attention waver for even a second

It is one thing to be an intense player, but another—and far more difficult—thing to bring that focus to coaching and manage to elicit that kind of high-powered play from your students. Yet every single woman who ever played for her

---

ANDY WHITEFORD *graduated from Loyola in 1987 after achieving All-American lacrosse status for three years. She was also a member of the U.S. lacrosse team and an assistant coach with and for Diane for six years. The mother of two young daughters, Andy possesses a master's degree and is currently teaching at a private school.*

responded to Diane's incredible energy and lived up to the unspoken demand, which she duly enforced: *Be your best, always!*

When I finally graduated, I couldn't wait to follow in her talented footsteps. I, too, became a graduate assistant and a teammate of Diane's once again. During those six years of coaching with her, I took in her unwavering desire to teach and help her team members grow in every aspect of their lives. I learned how much she cared about every member of the team and staff, without ever letting go of her intensity for the game. She cared about winning, sure, but never at the cost of her players' well-being. She wanted them to want it, and this desire took root in all her players, yielding amazing results.

Diane's intensity and ability to get her students to deliver results did not stop with lacrosse. After graduating from Loyola, she became a teacher. Several other players and I used to spend hours grading papers with her. I came across a phonics paper once on which a young student named Sam had answered every question incorrectly. Since this 0 percent accuracy rate was so unusual, I stopped and asked Diane if I should mark all the answers wrong.

"Whose paper is it?" she asked.

I read the name, and her expression suddenly changed.

"His paper is not supposed to be in that pile," she said. "Always give me his if you come across it again."

"Why?" I asked.

"It's a long story," Diane answered. "I'm pretty sure he's dyslexic, but his parents can't afford to have him tested. I work with him every day at recess to try to teach him learning strategies."

Now, I was teaching, too, and I knew that the break recess afforded was my most precious resource of the day— a time when I could recharge, relax, and grab some much-needed physical and mental replenishment. "Wow," I said, "when do you get to eat lunch?"

"I eat whenever I can fit it in, but right now it's more important to me that Sam learns how to read. He doesn't feel very good about himself, and I *will* teach him to read."

And she did. The intensity and determination she displayed helped pass the necessary skills to him. And I think that victory meant more to her than any game she coached that season.

As a seasoned teacher, I am reminded daily of that intensity. I remember how she was driven to push one little boy to strive, and how important improving his self-esteem was to her. There are many days when I am teaching that I am very tired, and it would be easy to neglect a child's needs. But all I need to do is think of Diane, and I am determined to make my students be the best that they can be.

Diane taught me that any task worth doing is worth doing to the best of my abilities. Her incredible energy and intensity inspires me every day, both in the classroom and out.

NEVER
JUDGE
ANYONE

CAROLYN'S STORY

When we were growing up, my sister Diane and I were taught to never judge anyone because you never knew when you might find yourself in that same situation. No matter what nationality, color, size, shape, or handicap, everyone was welcome in our home and lives without prejudice or judgment.

As a result of this, as a youngster Diane was drawn to people with handicaps. She accepted individuals for who they were, never even considering their appearance. One of these people was a wheelchair-bound boy, whom she referred to as her special friend, whose legs had been severed in a train accident.

Early in Diane's coaching career, while in a discussion with her players, she said, "You young people don't have passion for anything. When I was younger, I helped petition Baltimore City for wheelchair-accessible curbs on every street corner. To the contrary, you guys just attend college,

---

CAROLYN GEPPI, *an honorary assistant coach and Diane's sister, is a single parent to eighteen-year-old Jennifer and fifteen-year-old Paul. She resides in Greenland, New Hampshire, and owns a cleaning business.*

play lacrosse, and drink beer. You don't do anything for anyone else!"

Soon afterward, the Loyola Athletic Department invited the Maryland Ravens wheelchair basketball team to play the faculty, which included Diane. The only stipulation to the game was that the faculty also had to play in wheelchairs and by wheelchair basketball rules. The first team to score one hundred points was the winner. The Ravens spotted Loyola ninety-nine points, and by the end of the game, the final score was Ravens 100, Loyola 99.

After the game, Diane, who was still living at home at the time, approached our parents and asked if the Ravens team could come to our home for something to eat and drink. It was quite late, but they said, "Sure, why not." They mentioned, however, that there might be a problem since the house was not handicapped accessible. The team assured them that this would not be an inconvenience. After arriving by bus, they parked their wheelchairs outside, hopped up the steps into the house with ease, sat on the floor or in chairs, and had a great visit.

Upon leaving, they said they'd had a wonderful time because we didn't treat them as though they were handicapped. Diane looked beyond the handicap, seeing only a whole beautiful person. It was ironic that one day she would experience a similar situation: playing basketball with her kids in the backyard with one hand (her left side was paralyzed) and from a wheelchair, but always with a smile on her face and laughter in her voice.

"Now that I'm in a wheelchair," Diane would say to me, "I see how badly some people treat the handicapped. I'm glad we taught our kids to respect the less fortunate." She was very concerned that strangers shunned her because she was wheelchair-bound. One time, while waiting to get on an elevator, someone jumped in front of her and closed the doors. "Why are they ignoring me or just staring at me?" she asked. "They should have the courage to ask me what's wrong."

Throughout Diane's life, she was also an advocate for anyone who was different from the mainstream, including herself. When she was a child, she was the only girl on the boys' baseball team. Even if some in the community found this strange, she played her heart out undeterred. She instilled the same disregard for others' criticism in her children and her players. Her philosophy was: Do what makes you happy, no matter what others may think of you, and never be judgmental.

Diane was very popular with the boys outside baseball, too. They always wanted her to play with, hang out with, or date them. She could have gone with anyone she wanted to the various proms. One year, a boy much smaller than Diane asked her to his prom. Most girls at that age would have said, "No way!" But as usual, she saw people for who they were on the inside, and eagerly went to the prom with him.

Her classmates may have raised their eyebrows, but it didn't matter the slightest bit to Diane. To her, her date was wonderful. To her, everyone was wonderful.

Whenever I jump to a conclusion about people because of their appearance, I remember Diane's motto "Never Judge Anyone," and I hold back. I've met a lot of wonderful people that way, so thank you, Diane.

TREASURE FAMILY AND FRIENDSHIPS

MITCH'S STORY

When I think of Diane, the lessons she taught me about friendship and family always come to mind. I remember watching her coach with one of her children standing next to her and another sleeping in a backpack while she paced up and down the sidelines, coaching the team on to yet another victory. I was in awe of how easily she could balance her career with her family life.

On many occasions, Diane would bring one or all of her kids to work, practice, or the games. It was usually because of a school holiday, lack of a babysitter after school, or a sick day for one of them. From the time that they were infants crawling mischievously around her office and on the field, she would set them up in playpens, with coloring books and crayons, or with their homework assignments.

MICHELLE "MITCH" McDERMOTT-PACE *played at Loyola from 1985 to 1990. During her senior year, she was team captain and Unsung Hero. An elementary schoolteacher with a master's degree, Mitch also coached varsity and junior varsity lacrosse in the Ridley school district of Pennsylvania for ten years.*

On the field, the kids helped out by carrying sticks, chasing balls, and performing other odd jobs. Her oldest, Michael, would retrieve the heavier equipment and the watercooler, and carry out most of the manual labor. Her daughters interacted like little adoring sisters with me and the other players. The girls loved lacrosse and were often allowed to shoot at us on goal or get in the goal themselves during water breaks.

Yet with all her real family around, Diane still found the time to make my teammates and me feel as if we were a part of her family. In fact, having her family around only increased our feelings of attachment, and since many of us were far away from our own families, Diane's exposing us to her kids helped us to feel included. Aware of the need for us to feel like a unit, Diane encouraged the team to form strong bonds, bonds of friendship that really felt more like those of family members.

Diane wanted to make us a close-knit team who whole-heartedly supported each other, and she went about forging these bonds quite deliberately. At our morning practice, we had to run several miles around a nearby reservoir at 6 AM. We loudly cheered each other on to get through this run in the wee hours of the morning. Even if one of the girls came in last, we rooted her in and made her feel special for finishing the run and accomplishing her goal. It didn't matter how tired we were—Diane showed us that you find inner reserves of strength to cheer on your "family."

Diane knew the team was only a surrogate family, but she did her best to make it a strong surrogate. As a lacrosse player, you sacrifice a lot of things—spring break, for one. I remember we were in Virginia and feeling very homesick because we couldn't go home for Easter. A parent of one of the players and Diane's family had a surprise remedy prepared to cheer everyone up. They placed beautiful Easter baskets outside our doors! When we were about to leave our rooms the next morning, there they were. It was Diane's way to keep our minds focused on lacrosse—while throwing in some much-needed love, too.

Whenever our real families came to our games, Diane made time for them. She always took the time to chat with the parents who came from all over the East Coast. She made them feel comfortable and secure that their child was in such good hands. I remember seeing all of the moms, dads, siblings, and others on the sidelines laughing and having a great time. I thought, *This is what life should be— fun!*

Diane also taught us that friends and family help you stay grounded in life. They get you through the good times and the bad. When I injured my knee in the first game of my freshman year, I was devastated. Reconstructive knee surgery and a red-shirt season kept me out for two entire seasons. When I returned, I barely knew the team of almost all new girls, and here I was trying to recover my starting position. Diane gave me that chance, and the team followed her lead by cheerfully welcoming me back.

My first game with the "new" team was amazing. Everyone encouraged and supported me. My family and friends helped get me back in shape, and gave me the confidence to play again. In the years that followed, there were several players on the team who experienced the same knee fate that I had. In Diane spirit, I was one of many players who gave these girls the unwavering support they needed to overcome this adversity in their lives. I never questioned the need to carry on the tradition of love I'd received, for Diane taught us that when a family member is in need, your first duty is to come to her aid.

Diane and the team made me realize that family and friends should always come first in life. They should be number one on everyone's priority list. I have two daughters now, and Diane's strong message of love and support for friends and family is one of the most important lessons I wish to impart to them.

BE HAPPY EVERY DAY

SARA'S STORY

As the assistant director of athletic communication at Loyola College, I had the enviable responsibility of sharing Diane with the world, telling the media how wonderful she was, and then allowing them to share her with their audiences.

When I first came to Loyola, there were times I could be harsh, short with people, or easily saddened by problems in my life. But the moment I met Diane Geppi-Aikens and saw how she lived her life, all that changed. Di created an atmosphere that everyone wanted to be a part of and no one wanted to leave. Her team of more than thirty young women would be so quiet when she spoke, you could hear a pin drop. Everyone wanted to hear what this amazing creature had to say, whether it was advice, a story, a joke, or a command. Her mantra of "Be Happy Every Day" resonated

---

SARA DAY *is the assistant director of athletic communications at Loyola College. She works primarily with the women's basketball, lacrosse, and soccer teams. Originally from Elmira Heights, New York, Sara graduated in 2002 from Mansfield University in Pennsylvania, and is pursuing her master's degree in school counseling at Loyola College.*

throughout Evergreen, the name of the Loyola campus, and her senses of humor, fun, and adventure were legendary.

Many coaches I've worked with are serious types, to whom each snag in their carefully laid-out plans is a source of frustration. Not Diane. Every type of situation the team encountered could be remedied or joked about. "It takes so much more effort to dwell on the bad and stress over the little things than to let life happen for you," Diane often remarked. And she didn't just say it, she lived it.

Once we had problems with our bus as we were leaving our hotel in Syracuse before the Final Four, and were stuck for almost an hour. The clock was ticking away, our warm-up and practice minutes dwindling. Di just laughed. Here was the head coach of the number one seed in the national tournament "enjoying" getting stuck before the semifinal game.

There was no ranting and raving, not a single sign of irritation at the delay. Instead, entertaining stories emerged about the numerous times Diane's teams had gotten stuck before with bus trouble. She, her assistant coaches, and her dad, Pops, went back and forth, topping each other with hilarious stories as we all laughed. The funniest one was about when they'd had pizza delivered on the side of the road. When the driver announced that the bus was fixed, he had to repeat himself a few times to get through to the crowd of laughing players and coaches. No one enjoyed the moment more than Diane.

Even after our disappointing losses to Virginia and Princeton, Diane and the team were still positive and upbeat. "Enjoy the rest of the day! The game's over," she instructed. And the team did just that.

At the press conference following our devastating loss to Princeton at the Final Four, our photographer, Larry French, looked over at me with a very saddened face. Although I had allowed myself a brief tear at the close of the game, I told him to stop.

"Why?" he asked.

"Look at her," I said.

Diane was glowing. If you had looked up *happiness* in the dictionary at that moment, you probably would have seen one of the pictures Larry was now taking of her. As he snapped away, his own face changed to a smile as he saw her exuberance.

Later that night at our postgame party, the ESPN television crew asked me, "If this is the party when your team loses, what is the party like when you win?"

Everyone was genuinely delighted to be together and have a good time. Diane ordered a "dance-off" and Suzanne hit the floor twirling. It was unreal. At one point, I remember Di dropping her dinner plate in the lobby of the hotel and "accidentally" rolling over it with her new motorized wheelchair. Everyone stopped, concerned, until Di yelled, "Hey, that wasn't my fault. It was the brain tumor!"

I was thinking, *This woman has every reason to be at least a little bit sad. After all, she just lost what could have been a national title, she has a tumor growing on her brain stem, and she's in a wheelchair. But she's so happy just to be alive, sharing good times with those she cares about, that she can actually joke about her tumor. Who else would be capable of doing that?*

That was one of the profound moments when I realized that she was changing me. The rest of what I learned from her crept in over time, but at that moment, I knew my goal in life was to be that happy and that alive.

Diane's legacy shines through brilliantly in her children, who are all different and wonderful versions of their mother. I didn't meet Michael, the oldest, until Diane's viewing, but he was a pleasure. The next morning at the funeral, he hugged and consoled me the second he came in. And the day after that, Shannon, the youngest, opened the front door of her house to let in Janine Tucker, her mom's close friend for years and also Johns Hopkins's lacrosse coach. "Hello, Miss Janine," said Shannon. "Isn't it a beautiful day to be happy? And isn't my mom the best angel in the world?"

Toward the end of Diane's fight with cancer, she told a reporter that she felt lucky every day for what she had been blessed with: Despite her illness, she'd had amazing opportunities, met unbelievable people, and developed irreplaceable memories. She felt truly blessed by the life she had led and continued to lead up to her final days.

> I can honestly say that I now try my best to treasure each day I'm given; to follow Diane's example and see the humor in a disaster, the beauty in a rainy day, the potential in a hopeless situation. From Diane, I've learned to try to be as happy as she was, and to feel lucky every day.

EPILOGUE

······❖······

Following a long and valiant fight with cancer, Diane Geppi-Aikens died on June 29, 2003.

After spending much of her final months gently preparing her friends, players, and family for her death, Diane felt ready to go. In true Diane fashion, however, she handpicked several of her trusted friends to deliver eulogies at her funeral. To her friend Janine Tucker, Diane's disciple and head women's lacrosse coach at Johns Hopkins University, fell the honor of reading Diane's own carefully worded final message to Diane's beloved family, friends, and past and present teams.

On July 3, 2003, this is what Janine read:

> I wanted to speak last because the words I have to share with you are not my own. They are Diane's. I knew that Kristin, Betsy, and Dave would have wonderful things to say about Diane, so I asked Diane to speak to you through me. I told her I

would be honored to share her thoughts with you, and she loved the idea. And, as usual, she knew exactly what she wanted to say:

To my loving family, my amazing children, my dearest friends, and my true soul mate, know that you will always have an angel by your side watching out for you in all that you do, reminding you to believe in brighter days, finding ways for your wishes and dreams to come true, giving you hope that is as certain as the sun. This angel will give you strength, love, comfort, and courage. Know that you will always have an angel by your side, someone there to catch you if you fall, encouraging your dreams, inspiring your happiness, holding your hand, and helping you through it all. This angel will give you gifts that will never, ever end. This angel is someone wonderful to love and confide in. This angel will always keep your secrets, and will love you no matter what. You will always have an angel by your side to give you rainbows after every storm, to give you smiles through the tears, and to hold you in her heart, keeping you safe and warm. Know that you will always have an angel by your side, and that angel is me. I loved you all with everything I had in me. To my mom and dad,

I cannot put into words how much you mean to me. Know that every ray of sunshine that hits your face is a hug from me to you. To my team, you gave me a season to remember. There are *no* regrets, only tremendous pride. Thank you for playing your hearts out for me. I love you all. To *all* of my players, past and present, promise me you'll always remember what a special person *you* are. Promise me you'll hold on to your hopes and constantly reach for the stars. Promise me you'll live with enthusiasm and happiness over the years. Promise me that when you think of me it will always be with a smile. Promise you'll "remember when . . . ," and you'll always "look forward to . . ." Promise you'll do the things you've always wanted to do. Promise me you'll cherish your dreams and enjoy life day by day. Above all, promise to remember me and these wishes I have for you. I wish you all a life of love, and joy, and dancing. And may all of your dreams come true. To those whose lives I've touched in one way or another, know that I loved every day I had on this earth. Know that I am happy and safe. Know that I will always be a part of your life for as long as you'll have me in it. To all of you, I ask for one thing: Enjoy life to the fullest. You never know when it will be taken away from you.

Janine closed with:

> Diane, on Sunday, June 29th, I know I lost a friend, but I take great comfort in knowing I gained a guardian angel. I miss you so much already. You taught me to never, ever give up, to keep fighting for what I believe in. Thank you for being my friend, my mentor, and my hero. I will never forget you. I am a better person for having had you in my life. Good-bye, Diane.

Truly lucky every day of her life, Diane Geppi-Aikens will never be forgotten.